Boost Your Men

Memory Aids and Enhancem
Sharpen Your "Wits"

Dueep Jyot Singh

How to Series

Mendon Cottage Books

JD-Biz Publishing

Download Free Books!

http://MendonCottageBooks.com

All Rights Reserved.

No part of this publication may be reproduced in any form or by any means, including scanning, photocopying, or otherwise without prior written permission from JD-Biz Corp Copyright © 2016

All Images Licensed by Fotolia and 123RF.

Disclaimer

The information is this book is provided for informational purposes only. The information is believed to be accurate as presented based on research by the author.

The author or publisher is not responsible for the use or safety of any procedure or treatment mentioned in this book. The author or publisher is not responsible for errors or omissions that may exist.

Our books are available at

1. Amazon.com
2. Barnes and Noble
3. Itunes
4. Kobo
5. Smashwords
6. Google Play Books

Download Free Books!

http://MendonCottageBooks.com

Table of Contents

Introduction 4
Sensory Memory 13
"Reaffirmed" Memory and Fleeting Memory 15
Working Memory 16

10% of Brain Working – Totally False Myth 19

Factors Affecting Your Memory 22
Alcohol Consumption 23

Medicines and Drugs 24

Long-Term Memory 27
Auditory and Visual Memory 30
If I Could Do It, Surely You Can 42

Auditory Memory practice 51

Conclusion 53
Author Bio 58
Publisher 69

Introduction

What have I forgotten to do now?

Once upon a time, people used to boast about their long memories, especially when they were talking about the transgressions of other people, and they could recount clearly every word spoken and what happened next, about things which happened more than half a decade ago.

But most of us, today are rather proud of the fact that we are so absent minded, we forget so easily, and we put on our apologetic faces and say, uh oh, I forgot.

This is definitely not using our brains to the full capacity and this is why this book is going to tell you all about really good tips and techniques in which you can boost your memory.

So if you find yourself not able to recount the name of a once a dear friend, even though you can visualize his or her face clearly, or you forget the code of your credit card, or you find yourself looking rueful and saying that your memory is not what it once was, a bit too often, it is time you stopped doing that.

There is absolutely no cause to panic, if you find yourself forgetting things occasionally, but if it is a regular feature, in your life, and you have got the affectionate nickname of *Where-Are-My-Car-Keys,* a little bit of effort now, and some training exercises and you are soon going to find your memory boosted up surprisingly well.

What is the reason why so many people find that they memories are failing, especially when they do not seem to find any sort of reason for this to happen? Forget about the idea that a person, when he reaches his sixties is automatically going to start losing his memory, concentration capacities, and other powers of memory retention. This is just a stupid idea being promulgated by people who want to sell you memory booster tonics.

Imagine the brain to be a mass of muscles and tissue. It is made up of a large number of compartments, in which each portion is being used for some special purpose, the purpose for which nature has designed it. The more you use one particular portion, the more it is going to develop. On the other hand, if you stop using another portion of your brain, apart from it being a thorough waste of such prime potential, you are making sure that that tissue and muscle has deteriorated through sheer disuse.

And that is why, 20 years later, we just look at the ceiling, and say, now then, guys, do you remember, what was her name, you know that one who always used to wear those red shoes with blue socks, she made such a clown of herself, but she thought that she was such a fashion plate, – and other such instances. We can visualize her wearing those red shoes with the blue socks and still feel amused by it. But we cannot remember her name. That is because our visual "power" is stronger than our retentive memory.

And then suddenly someone says, yes, her name started with an S was not it or was it with an M? And then all of us begin to wonder what her name was. Half an hour later, when somebody's talking about a different subject together, someone immediately says, yes, her name was Tamara J. Tamara J. with the blue socks and red shoes. Triumph. How did somebody remember her, he remembered an instance, when she was wearing a virulent shade of light and sky blue, clashing with Navy and dark blue, and somebody just happened to comment that she really looks like a Blue Jay, no pun intended. And all of us had laughed.

Hurray, we have finally remembered her. And we can "see" her chirping about in the office, with that pink polka dot purse clashing horrendously with an orange and green outfit.

So remember that most of our memory is visual. But the person who remembers the story about the Blue Jay has an aural memory predominant. Also something here, we can remember colors and associate them with memories. So we are now going to learn a series of techniques, and tips, which are going to help you sharpen up your memory well and boost up your concentration powers.

What do you mean you forgot, I have noticed you have begun forgetting a bit too often, ever since you started hanging out with that female, what is her name, Sally, Sunny, Susie, Sadie, whatever.

Golly, Mom, her name is Tina. But you couldn't remember, could you.

Remember that memory loss can be temporary, or permanent. It is also going to depend a lot on your age, state of health, and gene line. Also, there are some races all over the world, whose minds are predominantly geared towards one particular activity, which is going to bring about all the differences between survival and possible destruction. This is a natural phenomenon, coming down through the millenniums.

That is why, in Africa and in many other parts of the world where life is still not very civilized, there are so many tribes, where they can smell out a stranger. I remember one of my Army friends telling me that the biggest mistake he made was taking his reconnaissance troop in one of the trouble areas with survival packs packed up with a number of items, along with that, someone had suggested shaving cream!

So here were the soldiers, shaving away because even in the jungle, they needed to look really spick and span for matters of morale, and they went washing that cream and their faces in the water source nearest to them. Their "opponents" could smell them from 400 yards! Apart from that, all they had to do was stand near the water source, and look for a twirl of something unusual in the water, – shaving cream foam. When the slaughter rate began to grow very high, somebody told them that they needed to do a reality check because they were not Playing Defenders of the Universe rushing in where angels feared to tread!

So now that we have spoken about natural inherited memory and how it is going to be adapted according to the circumstances in which a person finds himself, let us talk about some more factors, which are going to affect your memory.

For a long time, researchers working on the functioning of the brain have been experimenting on how a person remembers, and keeps his brain cells working normally and healthily.

Let me give you my take on this point. There is one major center, in which all the memories, feelings, emotions, instincts, and natural adaptations which allow a human being to survive are stored. Your brain is going to make sure that after the registration of any sensory perception, your brain registers that particular activity somewhere and makes a connection somewhere else.

All the different areas of your brain are connected together with neurons, which are part of your nervous system. Any stimulus of any kind is going to pass through the neurons in a fraction of a nanosecond and reach your brain.

That is the reason why once you touch a hot pan, unknowingly and the memory of that unpleasant results passes through your skin to reach your brain center.

The motor nerves are going to send this memory/result of this particular action to the brain. Along with that, the brain is immediately going to give a coordinated response which is lightning fast and instinctive to that particular area which has been harmed, to get away from the hot pan and do not touch it again under pain of potential harm.

Now once you have had the experience, it is going to be stored away forever, under this particular reference – touching a red hot pan or anything, which is heated is going to result in an immediate unpleasant burn. Conclusion, a once burned child dreads the fire.

I was reading a historical book about Native Americans, – written somewhere in the late seventeenth century – which was fascinating reading. The grandmothers used to take care of the children and the writer of the book – she was then 8 years old – spoke about how surprised she was when she saw the grandmother not stopping the baby child from going towards the fire.

Her own mother, who was a civilized European would immediately have snatched the baby away from the fire and shouted as everybody around her, for allowing her baby to get burned. Notwithstanding the fact that the mother had allowed the child to approach a fire through sheer carelessness, but she would not blame herself for this lapse in concentration or responsibility.

On the other hand, the Native American grandmother said that down the ages, the people of the clan had to teach their babies to survive from day one. And that could only be done through experience. If the baby got burned, well, that was life.

The mother was so horrified at this bit of callousness that she stopped her white daughter from visiting the Savage heathens ever again.

This is the reason why so many of us have lost our instinct to survive. We have begun forgetting the skills, given to us through nature, through disuse. However, we would rather spend a large amount of money in survival camps to show off our survival tactics, which we have honed in about 6 weeks.

And when we come back to civilization, we do not know what to do with the skills we learned in the jungles, like finding food, water, listening for predators, and other important skills, which can make all the difference between the survival of the tribe and immediate extermination at the hands of a four-legged or 2 legged predator.

However, these survival skills have been filed away somewhere in the center of our memory. This is going to be remembered the moment we need that particular knowledge, sometime or the other in the future. It is going to be conscious or subconscious.

And that is where we come to conscious and subconscious memory.

Sensory Memory

Any sort of motor skill, which you have learned once upon a time, and used your muscles physically to do it, is going to be stored away in your brain, as a sensory memory. That is why you can still shoot baskets even after 4 years, without having practiced. This is where your hand eye brain coordination comes into play.

I have not driven a car since I was 16. But I knew how to drive, – getting my drivers license on a rather powerful 52 HP, 4200 RPM Ambassador Car and about a decade ago, I needed to drive somewhere in an emergency. The moment I sat down behind the steering wheel, it was as if instinctive muscular and tissue memories had taken over, – and you can call this implicit memory.[1]

That is why you are never going to forget how to swim, ride a cycle, or any other activity, which you have done physically. Once this has been done a couple of times, the mind stores away the sequence of actions to receive a positive result. You can call them motor memories or automatic memories. It is also the base of a phenomenon so dear to teachers and even to advertisers of what is done subconsciously.

---

[1] And the moment I found myself humming Madonna's Tears on My Pillow, after 5 minutes of driving, – hey, this car was really light, you can relax now, you can handle it. It is not like an Ambassador – I told myself, why I had stopped myself from doing this pleasant activity, all these decades. But I still do not drive. However, I am reassured by the fact that if I have to, I can just pick up the car keys and drive away into the sunset, singing, I am a poor lonesome cowboy and far away from home! So one can only be thankful to the implicit memory of physical activities which is our natural inheritance.

"Reaffirmed" Memory and Fleeting Memory

I think I remember putting my keys in my pockets?!?

Our visual memory is spontaneously captured through an image and it relates to something else the moment it appears before us. The mind is going to take this particular memory along with the association, it threw up before us, on the appearance of that particular image and that is how your visual memory increases and grows strong.

That is the reason why the moment our teacher at kindergarten showed us the picture of a cat, all of us said meow and laughed! And that is because a teacher made that noise, when she showed us that particular picture. If we see that particular photograph anytime down the ages, the memory associated with that is us saying meow, and laughing, at the age of 3, those were the days, my friend!

So all the memories that you are going to have are going to be associated with something good, something bad, something nostalgic, or perhaps they may be wiped out of your memory store, because you did not need them at all.

Working Memory

Working memory is the base of the registration of all the information gathered by the brain from nanosecond to nanosecond. If it is unconscious, it is going to be subconscious. All these methods of information are going to be in symbolic form – words, objects, numbers, or anything else which can be stored away properly.

These are the "informational symbols," which have to be repeated again and again in order to reinforce your working memory . Otherwise the information will be forgotten in 15 seconds and will not be able to register itself in the long-term memory.

So now we come to why memories are wiped out. If that particular memory and its immediate association is not reinforced, it being a short-term flash in the pan, is going to be erased from your memory banks. And if during the years, it is not taken out occasionally, and remembered for a couple of minutes, it is going to give it to another fresher/more recent memory.

In the same way, if you are doing one particular action unconsciously without any sort of reinforcing and getting your brain to store it in the memory bank, it is possible that it is going to go into the short term memory storage portion of your brain. And the duration of that particular memory's existence is going to be less than one nano second.

This is the memory which you are going to be cudgeling and trying desperately hard to recall, but as your brain did not reinforce it, when it was being stored away, it considered it unimportant. And so it was wiped out.

You may want to try out this experiment for yourself. Look at something fleetingly. If your mind has not associated anything with it, think of that thing after half an hour. You are going to be in a state of "D-uh. What pink elephant? What made you think of a pink elephant?"

Unfortunately, this particular memory system is so fleeting, so natural and instinctive that many times you do things instinctively, and the mind does not register the fact, even though your muscles and tissues are working in the same way they have been doing – automatically, for a long while.

That is why your mind isn't going to register that particular fact, that you picked up your phone from the table, and put it in the cupboard, before you went for a walk. That was because you were in a hurry. Otherwise, your instinctive memory sequence of activities worked somewhere on this pattern – pick up your phone, slip it in your pocket, slip on your jogging shoes, leave for your walk, go outside in the park, listen to your music, and come back home.

During all this while, when you were walking, your brain was subconsciously and consciously overloading itself with new memories, being gathered together through all your 5 senses, and all your activities, including communications with the people you met, and other normal activities of the brain, being stored away in the memory center.

But this particular putting away of the phone activity was unusual – that of putting your phone in the cupboard and you did not give your brain the time to register that particular activity and reinforce it. So when you come home, after having remembered that, hey, you went for a walk, and oh gadzooks, where did you drop your phone, you absent-minded nitwit, were you listening to it, when you walked out of the door, naturally it is stress and tension time.

This is when you begin to go back to the sequence of actions. What did you do before you went out for a walk? Aaah-um, put on my shoes?

How do I know, I am asking you, yells your brain, think, you dim bulb, think.

Aaah-um, put on the phone in my pocket? Your brain does not let up. It is still calling you bad names.

You begin to feel frazzled. You begin to feel hassled. You want to sit down and put your hands between your head, because you cannot remember, cannot remember. Our brain is so tired. We are getting stressed out. Why cannot we remember?

If you had just taken 1 minute to reinforce the command from your brain to your hand – listen, I am picking up my phone and I am going to put it in the cupboard here, and you had better remember it, I am not going to take it out in the rain, or any other reason, – see you have done a little bit of talking, or association here and the brain is going to remember this.

And when you come back home, you are going to pull your phone out of the cupboard, check your messages, and have absolutely no tension.

So moral of the story, learn how to activate your brain in such a manner that all the actions you do should be associated with something firm for at least 25 seconds, – which is going to reinforce the memory in your brain.

Fleeting memory is less than 10 seconds. So when you say, I have a fleeting memory that I did this, it means your brain was registering somewhere that you mutt, you put your phone on top of your jewelry box in your cupboard, so remember it.

If you remember the fleeting memory well and immediately it associates it with Ahah- jewelry box, phone, there you are, you are already strengthening your memory.

10% of Brain Working – Totally False Myth

One does not know about the full capacity of the brain and how much it can assimilate, but the more you use it, the more strength it is going to get.

Now here I am going to bust a myth where some researcher wanting to look important started up some stupid theory that we are using just 10% of our brains. That is so not true. Human beings like all other animals are using hundred percent of their brains, consciously and subconsciously. If 90% of the brain was not being used, you would be a vegetable, because that means it was not doing its normal work of keeping your body functioning properly, thinking up something else to do, right now, subconsciously, while unconsciously, you are making up the right sentence which is going to make the meaning come through, and so on.

What is my brain doing right now? An onlooker is going to say, well, she is sitting down and getting the words down on paper. That is what he sees consciously. Unconsciously and naturally, the work of the brain is never ended. It is visualizing the next sentence, but subconsciously, it is working 24/7, keeping my blood circulation, nervous system, sensory system, and other systems working normally, while giving out other output, from nanosecond to nanosecond. The brain does not work in normal measurements of time. It works in superfast lightning natural time, which cannot be measured by human beings. And that is why; sometimes it registers something, before that thing is apparent to you, visibly, physically, mentally, emotionally, or spiritually.

That is how living beings have survived, with your brain working at 2 levels simultaneously – look at the computer, and correct that typo. This is what my brain is doing, consciously, at this particular moment.

At the same time, there is some message going somewhere through the nervous system that hey, you, your nose has been itching for the past nanosecond, you had better scratch it and alleviate that not so amusing sensation.

And then you send back a message to the brain, in acknowledgment, of course, of course, it is itching, but I am too busy at the moment, with both my hands occupied.

Now the brain is definitely not going to leave it at that. It is going to give you an order to itch your nose a bit, and scratch it against the rough surface of your sweater/fabric on your shoulder. So you do it.

What gave the brain the idea to use that particular method of alleviating that itching proboscis? The brain is just using common sense because it is definitely never going to sit idle. That is why it is going to use all the knowledge gathered through experience, to come up with a logical solution, – rough fabric – nose within reach – rub nose on fabric. That is that!

If 90% of the brain is not working, Mr. Vegetable, I am sorry, but you would be totally paralyzed, because that meant 90% of your sensory systems had atrophied and become defunct. When a person suffers from a stroke, 10% or 20% of his brain is not working and that is the one particular area which has malfunctioned.

Unfortunately, brain cells are the only cells in the body which do not rejuvenate, unlike the rest of the cells. So once they are destroyed, the tissue is dead and gone forever.

However, with a little bit of exercise on your brains, you are going to make sure that this tissue never gets defunct, ever.

Factors Affecting Your Memory

Your age, bad diet, weakness, stress, a bad digestive system, and insomnia are just some of the factors which are going to affect the working of your brain.

Apart from this, it is natural that to keep in good health, you need to have a healthy mind in a healthy body. Here are some detrimental factors which are going to upset the normal working of your brain, and of course an excess of these items are going to change the normal physiology of the brain. In such a manner that it is going to have a negative hold on your brain on a long-term basis.

Alcohol Consumption

On a short-term basis, consumption of alcohol has a detrimental effect on your physical equilibrium, modifies your attention, your perception, and your judgment. On a long-term basis, it is going to alter the natural nerve terminations in your nervous system, so that the neurons do not function properly.

The neurons are linked to each other, with nerve cells, nerve tissue, nerve fibers, and terminations. But when they get altered with the help of plenty of alcohol consumption, this is going to have a deleterious effect upon the brain.

Medicines and Drugs

I was just watching Kindergarten Cop and began to think about a particular rather obnoxious character in it. This was this mother Eleanor Crisp who took a perfectly healthy son, and began feeding him medicines and drugs, since he was a child in order to *prevent him from falling sick.*

Who thought that one up?

That little boy grew up to be hooked on drugs, without which he could not function normally, sensibly or logically.

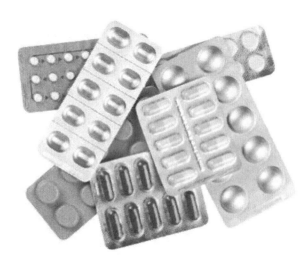

By the time the child reached his twenties, he was perfectly [2]mad. That was because his perfectly normal brain had stopped functioning properly,

---

[2] https://www.youtube.com/watch?v=O5KvtrFgg0k – you can skip the violent parts but just see this to analyze the effect of drugs fed to children, all in the name of this is for your own good…

because the mother in all her all pervading I-know-it-all,-and-I-know-exactly-what-I-am-doing-is-right-for-my-child-and-what-the-good-of-my-child sense of righteousness had messed up his natural bio physiological functions with poisonous drugs.

So are you feeding your child drugs, and medicines, which he definitely does not need, just because your doctor has said that it is going to keep them healthy and strong? Or are you feeding them, these drugs and medicines so that they do not fall sick or suffer from any sort of infection?

I am sorry to say, but you have already begun poisoning your child and have become responsibility for the loss of his future brainpower. That is because diet has – especially in the initial stages of life – a great deal to do with the development of the brain.

And instead of feeding him healthy, nourishing food, you kept on feeding him drugs and supplements, because it was the fashionable thing to do/somebody advised you to do that/you thought that one up yourself/well, God help your poor little helpless child because you are not helping him.

These medicines are going to include antidepressants, antibiotics, and also a number of anti-inflammatory drugs, antihistamines, sleeping pills, and relaxants. These are going to make your brain "go to sleep", and that means memory loss in the future.

In ancient times, drugs like opium, poppy and other drugs were used only for medicinal purposes and were never used as recreational drugs. The idea of recreational drugs came into existence in the late nineteenth century, when Europeans decided to use opium as a product to export to Asia and the Orient. And from Europe, the idea spread to America, especially during the

World Wars, the Great Depression, Vietnam and Korea, when drug smuggling into America from Asia became a multibillion dollar industry.

In the 1960s, cocaine as a recreational drug was considered not to be addictive, because according to its users, it cleared the brain and helped a person think clearly.

Sherlock Holmes unfortunately is a 100% cocaine addict.[3] Dr. John H Watson knows that. So does Sir Arthur Conan Doyle. In Victorian times, and before, doctors used opium under the name of laudanum, and cocaine extract in order to help a person relax, especially if he was injured or he had undergone any sort of mental, physical or emotional trauma.

Thus you got laudanum addicts.

When they took cocaine, their brains naturally worked in mysterious ways, and that is how they supposedly solved problems. But when they did not have anything else to occupy them, they showed all the symptoms of drug addicts with their hyperactivity, inability to sit quietly, or do something constructive, bad mood swings, bad temper, and other aftereffects of long-term drug abuse on an otherwise healthy brain.

---

[3] I was laughing at these practical statements by Dr. John Watson in Sherlock Holmes's latest episode – The Abominable Bride when Sherlock takes a drug trip and Dr. Watson asks him – *are you sure it is still a 7% solution that you take* ? And once when he replies to Sherlock's question of – "since when have you had any imagination?" and his answer is "perhaps since I convinced the reading public that an unprincipled drug addict is some kind of gentleman hero."

Long-Term Memory

This is the memory which is most important of all, and most significant. It is going to analyze the episodic memory and needs constant stimulation in order to function properly. This is where you need continuous memorization and enforcement of this power packed weapon, in order to keep it healthy and functioning in its natural manner.

Compared to short-term memory, a long-term memory always has a longer lasting effects, especially when you have used it once or twice during your lifetime and reinforced it.

Your long time memory is going to make its base right in the beginning of your existence. From moment one itself, every single thing happening to you is going to be stored away in your brain because it is a tabula rasa – an empty slate on which things are going to be written for the next 9 years, when your brain develops as you develop.

By the age of 9, the brain had developed most of its faculties, and it would keep developing in the same path which had been trained during these years. This is where the child was exposed to all the different sensory perceptions. He learned to use his ears to understand what was being said. At the same time, he saw something which would associate the hearing and the visual activity and that would be registered in his brain. Thus, picture of the cat/meow.

Unfortunately, in our day and age, we have forgotten one of the most powerful senses of them all, the sense of smell. If I tell you, visualize the color blue, you are immediately going to close your eyes, and there, in your mind's eye, you can see the color, perhaps the blue of the sky or perhaps the dark blue of a garment.

But if I tell you to bring up the smell of petrol or frying bacon or the pages of an old book, you are going to be hard put to do that. That is because human beings have lost the power of visualizing/bringing up the sense of smell down the ages.

On the other hand, just the aroma of frying bacon, water sprinkled on dry earth, or a pleasant perfume can bring up another memory, a nostalgic one, a happy one, and it is going to be something associated with that particular memory, possibly in childhood and related to all your 5 senses or perhaps your instinct.

If you enjoy eating, the memory of pleasant food being cooked is going to conjure up an associated memory of picnicing with your friends in the sun with plenty of beer and sun. This is how brains associate memories with other memories, sights, taste and smells.

The first 9 years is the most important age in the lifetime of a child when in ancient times, children were trained to develop their brains and all their faculties to the best of the ability of their teachers.

This is where they learned visually, orally, audibly, through their senses and through what they saw and learn to analyze. Nowadays, scientists are talking about 2 types of important memories, – auditory and visual.

Auditory and Visual Memory

In fact, brains would rather keep pleasant memories when given a choice, to take the place of unpleasant memories.

Remember that not all of us are going to have our major memories hundred percent auditory or hundred percent visual memories. However, most of us have one particular memory type that is better developed than the other. Nevertheless, all of us have a mixed type memory, depending on the situation.

I am now going to give you a test, in which you are going to find out whether your auditory memory or your visual memory is more predominating at the moment. This is more of a psychological test, but it can give a background about which particular memory portion of your brain acts quicker, when you have been given an order to complete something requested of you by your brain.

Please be frank, when you are completing this test. After all, you do not want to hide your own personality from yourself! Take a piece of paper and pencil, and tick the right column from 1 to 20.

	Always	Often	Sometimes	Never
I always comprehend what somebody is telling me				

When I have a problem, I tried to find the solution as soon as possible.				
I have the need of appreciation and approval of all the people around me.				
I like watching TV when I am doing some other activity.				
I am discouraged by failure or the mere idea of failure.				
I like reading books and other journals in print.				
I am not very happy with other people				

giving me orders.				
I am very particular about details.				
I do not find myself comfortable in unforeseen situations or instances. I cannot deal with them.				
Visual First impressions of the things I see or the people I meet are very important to me.				
I am hyperactive. I cannot relax for a moment without getting up or doing				

something or the other.				
I am rather impatient.				
I like things to be explained concisely, precisely, clearly and systematically.				
I am very careful about my looks and general appearance.				
I like my life well-regulated and everything done at fixed hours.				
I am a bit worried when I think about the future.				
I have need to				

feel myself useful, all the time, and needed by others.				
I lose my interest or concentration very fast.				
I talk impulsively and spontaneously, what I think.				
I do not respond very well to any sort of criticism, at any time, from anybody.				

Now that you have truthfully completed this psychological table you are going to count your score. At the end of the test, you are going to give yourself 4 marks for every Always, 3 for every Often, 2 for every Sometimes, and a 1 for every Never.

Remember that there is no hard and fast rule for the ticking of these questions. It may depend on your mood and on the circumstances and on how truthful you are feeling at the moment.

Naturally, there is nothing like 100 percent auditory memory or hundred percent visual memory, but like I said before, it is going to depend on you on how you evaluate your personality and memory profile, and after having calculated your score, you look at the best way in which you can boost up your memory.

More than 50 points

If you have more than 50 points, you have a visual memory. You have the need to see something before you memorize it. And when you try to remember something, you would rather prefer seeing a design, scheme, or words to explain things better to you rather than long winded explanations. When you are in the presence of other people, you pay more attention to the manner in which they talk to you, and their attitudes, the expression on their faces, to their gestures and other visual factors which are stored away in your memory and associated with those particular gestures on that particular event or moment.

This type of memory reminds me of learning devices used by our teachers as a child. England was painted pink, France green, America red, China blue, and so on. Even so many years later, whenever I think of these dominions, I always associate them with their respective colors as remembered on the map!

When I was a lecturer, training Degree students in the management, tourism, and service industry sectors, all of us faculty members worked on visual presentations rather than long winded explanations in order to teach our classes. We use LCD projectors to project our PPT presentations which we made ourselves, onto a widescreen and with every slide we gave a clear and concise explanation of the information given on the slide.

Each of these presentations had colorful illustrations, explanations of just a couple of words, points, or sentences. We would then allow the students to look at the slides, for a couple of seconds, and then begin our clear and concise explanations. We were encouraged to use music and cartoons in order to reinforce the visual memory.

This was in 2003, and we were the first Inst. in our State to start this way of teaching. It was something unique and pioneering at that particular time and I often had other faculty members from other colleges, universities, and institutes dropping in, very often into my class, as well as those of my colleagues, just to look at our methodology of teaching and why we got hundred percent results! And we also had to train other instructors on how best they could improve the success rates of their particular students in this state-of-the-art manner of teaching.

Incidentally, if we did not have any class to take, we were given full permission by our boss, Major S, to attend the class of any of our colleagues, so that they were kept on their toes because they were also teaching their peers their own particular subject. This was an excellent association of visual memory with auditory memory, and everyone was thrilled with this method of teaching. Also, we were increasing our own knowledge base, so that we could take over their classes, if by any chance the lecturer did not turn up. Farsighted boss, ours! Very nice, and very popular because he encouraged us to spread our wings and not limit ourselves to just one field of knowledge, our particular field.

After the class was over, the PowerPoint presentations went straight into the library so that all the students could gain access to this permanent fountain of knowledge.

How to reinforce this memory. You will need to repeat the visuals in your mind again and again to store them away. People with a visual memory predominantly have the habit of saying, I am going to try to remember this tomorrow. You have to bring up a visual memory by noting down the important points of your agenda visually, so that you can remind yourself of what needs to be done, when, and how.

Less than 50 points

You have an auditory memory.

You are going to have a better understanding of something, if you can hear it clearly, long, and loud. In fact, if you hear anybody complaining about something on these lines that she has to be told, for her to understand what needs to be done, you just need to tell them that that particular she has an auditory memory, and visual memory aids are not going to work so efficiently or effectively for her.

For this, you have need to repeat things, loudly, in order to fix the memory of that particular thing in your mind. That means you can try by repeating poems, your phone number, your credit card number, loudly, long, and clear to memorize it, and above all, to remember and understand it.

For people with these sort of memories, you want the instructions to be concise and precise. They are going to lose their interest and you their attention if you keep talking about nonessentials.

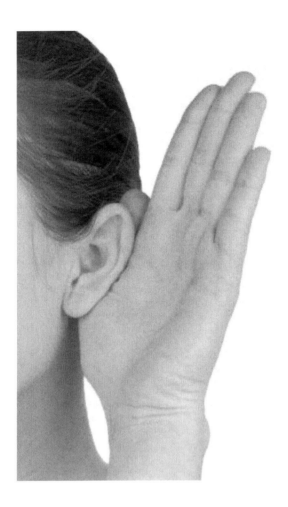

This reminds me of a really amusing instance, when a relative was talking about his experiences in the Army with "batmans". "Batmans" are a British Army tradition, – coming down from the Napoleonic Wars – where officers in the Army were given the help of a soldier who would help take care of their kit, wake them up in the morning, get them ready for parades, and office and do all the duties of a servitor to his officer.

So uncle was talking about why he preferred Batmans of one particular region. According to him, once you give them an order, they would follow them precisely and concisely, until you told them otherwise. Often they used their own initiative to make things easier for you.[4]

On the other hand, he said, affectionately, that there were other young lads, from other regions, who used to appear every evening and say, "Sir, you gave the instructions for this morning, last night. Do I have to repeat the same instructions tomorrow morning too?" In the most innocent manner.

Excellent example of auditory memory! Reinforcement through clear and concise instructions, given often, and given precisely. It is not that these sort of people have a short-term memory, they just like hearing things being said, so that they can remember them. People with such auditory memories are also capable of recounting every word you told them precisely, which is rather hilarious.[5]

---

[4] One fine day, uncle had to appear on parade, at 7:30 in the morning, and found his Batman waking him up at 7:15, instead of the usual 6:30 wake-up call with hot tea. The batman allowed him to sleep in, because he thought his officer had looked a bit tired the previous night. After Uncle had stopped yelling, the Batman just told him quietly, Sir, do not worry, have your breakfast at leisure, while I go and have a talk with the Commanding officer's Batman. He is going to lose his officer's socks, and uniform tie, and by the time they are going to be found, you will be in good time to join the parade! He did. At 8:15.

Where in the world can you get service like this from loyal batmans? No wonder, even after their officers retire, the serving Batmans ask to be assigned to them, to take care of them for the rest of their lives. My grandfather's Batman had this rather habit of talking to my grandfather in rustic language of my grandfather's village - thou and thee , while taking care of him, and scolding him for getting his feet wet , or not having that extra piece of fruit, he had cut just like one would do a recalcitrant child and then add an afterthought of Sir. He served my grandfather for 64 years, even after grandfather's retirement.

[5] "Sir, you said, wake me up at 6:30 sharp. While I am drinking my tea, you are going to lay out my uniform, see that my briefcase is packed with the files that I am working on, and also see that the hot water is ready for which you are going to

I also remember a D. E. Stevenson which I was reading, in which a young boss had a secretary with an auditory memory. He was dictating a letter to be sent to one of his clients who had sent him a letter which he was answering. And luckily he asked his secretary to read out the letter aloud at the end. She did –

It went something on the lines of, *regarding your proposal, Mr. Brown, I would like to inform you that, egads, this old man.... Has absolutely no idea about what he is talking about, does he think that we are going to agree to his absurd demands, our Board of directors have decided that...*

And so on went the letter.

And she noted everything down. *Including his asides.* Seriously, there are people like that. Just imagine what would have happened if he had not asked her to read out the letter aloud before typing out the final draft.

This is a clear case of people with auditory memories not thinking of what they have heard, because their minds are not assimilating and analyzing what is being spoken. They are just doing an automatic gesture of following the order of Take a Letter Miss XYZ, given to them by their boss!

---

switch on the geyser at 6 o'clock sharp. Breakfast should be ready by 7. Now repeat what I said."

"No, I meant, I asked you to repeat what I said."

"That is what Sir, I am repeating what you said."

Very logical. But somebody who had not been confronted with such precise reporting would be taken aback when he heard it for the first time. No wonder all of us broke into giggles/snorts – depending on our gender –, because all this was said in such an innocent manner and this was done every evening in every house!

Boost Your Memory

Anyway, these people need to repeat things out aloud, so that they can remember through their ears. According to them, they are going to understand better when they hear things.

How to reinforce this particular type of memory. This can only be done over time. When we were young, we were taught with an ancient way of teaching, which has come down the ages, for millenniums. That was continuous repetition.

This is how, by the age of 3 and a half and 6 and a half, we who had begun to repeat the multiplication table, every evening, in a sing song with our father ever since we were 2 and a half and 5 and a half, – I started late at 5 and a half, but father had to make sure that his baby son could at least speak/sing, we had our multiplication times table at our fingertips.

So when he used to ask us rapid fire questions like seven times seven? We used to sing back forty nine. That was because we had assimilated this knowledge through sound associations, instinctively.

This is just a small example. In ancient times, there were people who could sing out huge holy books, from memory. Even today, there are such people in the world. That is because they have been trained since childhood to repeat things, again and again, until the sound associations make the memory respond to what word comes next.

Also remember if you have this sort of memory, you will need to reinforce your clarity of thought and the sequence in which the words are going to flow. These people do very well especially when they need to speak on a particular topic, and once they have practiced and reinforced their memories, they are going to talk for a long while.

The only problem is that they cannot speak extempore. Any breaking off or any sort of interruption, and then they are in a quandary. That is because their flow of thought and memory has been interrupted. But I have this tip for such people. Repetition, loud and long and often. Do not wait for the last moment if you have an oral exam. If you have a speech to make tomorrow morning, make sure that you revise the speech once before you go to sleep. You are going to revise it again, first thing the next morning and you will have noticed that it was fixed in your mind, when you slept.

If I Could Do It, Surely You Can

Start him young… His brain is ready and receptive to take on brand-new experiences, because he is naturally geared and program to do so.

I am not joking about this. Believe it or not, there was a time, where in many parts of the world, children had extraordinary retentive powers because they were trained from childhood itself to observe, repeat, and speak, because their memories were so sharp and clear.

But nowadays, why have teachers forgotten about these methods of helping children memorize, through repetition? They are worried about loud noises! And what about visualization? What is that? Many teachers do not know.

Photographic Memory Practice

So here I am going to tell you all about how we learned about powers of observation, through constant practice. We were just average children, but thanks to parents, who made sure that we would not be allowed to slip into a state of intellectual mediocrity, we had really sharp powers of observation.

Even though researchers are going to say, that that is not possible, I tell you, that that is possible, every child is born with it. It is natural and inherent. All children need to do is get to know more about it. So do their parents.

One is the eidetic memory – also known as the photographic memory. Here we are going to talk about visualization. Like I told you before, consider your brain to be a white screen. Close your eyes. Try to imagine a scene. It should be vivid. It should have a number of colors. It should have a number of features like trees, flowers, and the blue sky.

Having difficulty, conjuring up such a visual feature? Do not worry, unless you have seen such a picture, or you have an unusually strong photographic memory, it is going to be difficult to conjure up such a picture in the initial stages.

Well, in that case, I am going to help you with your photographic memory.

You are going to look at this photograph carefully for exactly 2 minutes, because this is a rather complicated photograph . After that has been done, you are going to place a book on the photograph, covering it, and then close your eyes.

Now you are going to visualize the picture that you saw, in your mind's eye. Imagine that photograph. Do you see it as you fixed it in your memory, for the past 2 minutes? No peeping at the questions beforehand please?

In the initial stages, it is going to be a bit difficult to conjure up the image, in your mind, because you have allowed your visualization/photographic memory area to be neglected.

Now let us start with the question and answer session –

1. How many people are there in the photograph?

2. How many glasses are there on the table? What are the liquids they contain?

3. What is the color of the lampshade?

4. What is the boy in blue holding in his right hand?

5. How many books are there in the book rack? Extra points, if you can tell their colors.

6. How many boys and how many girls are there in this photograph?

7. How many packets of French fries are there in this photograph?

8. What is the color of the T-shirt of the girl sitting in the middle?

9. How many cushions can you see, and what color are they?

10. How many shelf boxes can you see behind the sofa? They are semi-hidden, but you can visualize how many they are.

Give yourself one point for every right answer and extra 2 points for amazing powers of observation and memory, if you got the fifth answer correct on both parts of the question.

In the initial stages, believe it or not many people get anywhere between 3 – 4 answers correct, because they have not learned how to visualize, and their photographic memories have not been reinforced, all this while, since childhood.

If you have learned something about the powers of observation, during your daily life, you are going to get anywhere between 5 - 8 correct. If you scored

9 – 10 correct means you have been training yourself, for a long while which is rather admirable.

This is how we did our training in visual photographic detail, when we were children, picking up pictures from books, especially those with plenty of emphasis on color, detail, and different activities going on in just one picture.

After that, you are going to do the practice session on this particular photograph, given below. Get somebody to look at the photograph and make a large number of questions to ask you, while you are remembering it. If they happen to be your siblings, or family members already annoyed with you – believe me, that can happen – get ready for really difficult questions like how many different types of vegetables can be seen on the right side of the table, how many plates are there on the table, how many strawberries are there on the fruit juice glass, what does the cocktail glass have, and how many of them are present in number, and all of these have to be done in 3 minutes.

Believe it or not, when I had to do this test for the first time to sharpen up my fading photographic memory, about 2 and a half years ago, I could not visualize this photograph in my mind's eye, when 20 years ago, it would have been right there, bright and clear with every detail etched.

But for 20 years, I did not use my photographic memory, and sad to say today I have lost the power of visualization. I am not going to blame age. I cannot blame alcohol, because I do not drink, but I am going to plead laziness.

Get set go. Extra points, if you counted the number of strawberries, around the chocolate vanilla gateau - bottom left, under the custard in syrup – which is excellent, because that means that your mind is totally geared to systematic detail. 89% of the people out there would not be so particular.

Now we come to the printed word.

This is also visual memory, because we are retaining the memory of symbols and words in our minds eye.

When we were little babies, we had Reader's Digest's The Great World Atlas, which was one of our favorite books. We used to spend hours over it after we came back from school, teaching ourselves all about the world, and the solar system. We never got to the stage of learning maps by heart, because that was a very scary idea, but we thought up a game of our own.

This is how you are going to play it. Remember, children are very inventive, and they love exploring new frontiers of knowledge as long as parents allow them plenty of initiative and leeway to do so. Once the thirst for knowledge has been put in a child, he should be left alone, to explore his surroundings, and assimilate memories, colors, and textures of the things around him. All of them are so miraculous.

Anyway, here are 2 photographs, of the particular pages that fascinated us the most – the Earth's Treasures.

After an explanation of the Earth's treasures, we could browse through all the elements, metals, and treasures found in the earth, with a little bit about them explained, along with the place on earth, where they were found the most often.

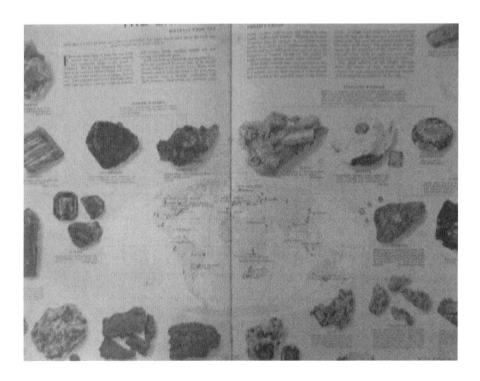

We took anywhere between 5 to 10 minutes to study both these pages and all these minerals, and then tossed a coin, to see who would go first. I and my younger sibling played this game, and the one who won would have a choice whether he covered a picture first or he described a picture first with a little fist covering any photograph on these 2 pages.

We had challenged our brains to learn this knowledge. We were honing up our observational and retentive memory powers of our own accord. These minerals included Galena, Fluorspar, gold, Sphalerite, asbestos, pitchblende, Torbernite, beryl, emerald, aquamarine, zircon, platinum, silver, sulfur, coal, graphite, Kaolin, Apatite, Pentlandite, quartz, Opal, Carnelian, Agate, Chrysophrase, Topaz, Olivine, sapphire, corundum, Ruby, bauxite, cinnabar, Malachite, Chalcopyrite , Azurite , sodium chloride, garnet, cat's-eye hematite, and feldspar.

How many adults know of these metals or are interested in them? Not many, unless they are mineralogist or geologists. But we found these particular pages, very interesting, and we had to read out the description under our sibling's hidden fists.

Well, let me admit it, my brother was rather clever, he always covered the minerals at the bottom of the page – the copper minerals – because he knew that I would not be able to memorize –

Chalcopyrite copper – iron – sulfite, crystals of chalcopyrite and quartz are shown. Most widespread and important ore of copper. Found in Northern Rhodesia.

That is because I was busy memorizing the minerals described at the top of the pages. So remember that your mind also prefers what to memorize first in preference to other things and how often.

So what you are going to do is look in your collection of books. You may have some book somewhere with colorful interesting photographs and interesting descriptions – for example, [taken from this page] *silver, specimen carries some milky white quartz used as an alloy with copper in coinage, plate and jewelry. Used in the electrical, photographic and chemical industries and in braising solders. Found in Mexico.*

You are teaching your brain to assimilate little bits of knowledge. You may want to read them out aloud. When we were at college, and all of us were together, studying for our exams, many of us used to escape to the college gardens, where we could not hear our fellow students memorizing chemical formula or scientific names of plants out aloud –Triti-cum Vulgare- Wheattttt, treeticum vulgaray- wheeet… T-r-i-t-i-c-u-m, can anybody lend me a piece of slate chalk?

At that time, we used to use the black slates and chalk pencils normally used by kindergarten students on which to write and practice our work. Come the exam season, and all the booksellers would stock up on boxes of slate chalk and slates, because every student wanted one/needed one. Also, we often found ourselves chewing on the chalk pencils to concentrate better. Sorry to say, they tasted really nice. That is one sensory taste, I remember and can recall!

Maybe we were suffering from calcium deprivation. We called it exam stress and tension. After our exams, our professors used to give us helpful household hints on how to get rid of the accumulated chalk in our stomachs, by eating tomatoes with black pepper, every night before going to sleep. That would at least get rid of the worms/parasites, in that chalk, if any.

I have not seen a black graphite slate or a chalk pencil for the last 35 years, alas. Where have they gone?

Auditory Memory practice

This was normally practiced by the bards, when they were talking about old stories. In ancient times, rhythm was all, so you are going to begin rollicking to this poem, which was one of my childhood favorites taken from "Topsy-Turvy Songs and Poems," written in the Seventies. We just loved it. Read it once or twice, and you are going to find yourself recalling it more than 3 decades later.

Along with this, we found Lochinvar also very easy to learn and remember. What a rollicking poem written by Sir Walter Scott.

Montezuma and his Puma
Mexican Legend by A. Passman
Montezuma
Met a Puma
Coming through the Rye:
Montezuma made the Puma
Into apple pie

Invitation
To the nation
Everyone to come.
Montezuma
And the Puma
Give a kettle-drum.

etc, etc, etc…

Here are some other examples –
The Ballad of East and West-

http://www.theotherpages.org/poems/kiplin01.html

Lochinvar-
http://www.poetryfoundation.org/poem/183947

Once upon a time, every student had to learn Casablanca and speak it out loud.

The boy Stood on the burning deck.

http://digital.library.upenn.edu/women/hemans/works/hf-burning.html

We were so tired of it, that we spoke our own version – *the boy stood on the burning deck, eating peanuts by the peck* and so on, even more rude imagery, but not in front of our teachers.

Conclusion

Of course, there are plenty of tests online, with which you can sharpen your memory, and wits, remember practice makes perfect, and I have given you just 3. So here is an interesting URLs, especially about one topic on which I have not touched – Mnemonics.

https://www.mindtools.com/memory.html

I remember as a child, our master teacher teaching us how to spell *Mathematics* as "He sits with 2 mats on his side, and his following words are ICS." We never got this particular spelling wrong! Mnemonics have been used down the ages, especially when you had to learn lists of scientific names.

This is also a very interesting page, so you may also want to use your imagination and think up mnemonics on your own.

https://en.wikipedia.org/wiki/List_of_mnemonics.

Do not ever tell a child, that he is not capable of remembering because he is a little child and he is burdening his tiny little brain. I have heard people saying this, and following it up with - He is just a baby.

Not only is this patronizing, but it is extremely stupid. In fact, the child has a much more powerful brain, than you have in all your adult smug superiority. You may have more experience, but he has more retentive power, and he still has the capacity to hone his powers to get a super brain.

Mozart began composing at the age of 5, and the world marveled, because they considered him to be a child prodigy. That is because they were teaching their children that the cat sat on the mat at the age of 5 and A was an archer who shot at a frog.

But in his family, it was taken for granted, that being surrounded by music, he would learn how to pick out chords on musical instruments because he had seen everybody doing that, and he was doing that at the age of 3. By the age of 4, he had learned how to play short pieces and by the age of 5, his brain had already started associating words and music together to compose concertos!

This is true.

Today, we are preventing our children from reaching their full potential, because we have bound them and limited them, to our own notions about what we think is right for their age group.

Seriously speaking, I find this very ridiculous, especially when I saw a teacher/colleague snatch away the Swiss Family Robinson, being read by a six-year-old child and giving her little Red Riding Hood to read.[6] That was appropriate subject matter for the child to read, according to this knowledgeable pedagogue. That was what she had been taught during her Bachelor of Education Degree training.

When I told her that I was on to Charles Dickens at the age of 6, and that was very admirable that the child's parents had used a little bit of initiative, and taught her to read and appreciate books like the Swiss Family Robinson, her answer was – well, they wrecked your brains and you are totally

---

[6] I was undergoing 3 months practical training under a supervisor to obtain my Bachelors of Education Degree to teach school children, even though I was already a College lecturer. Everybody should have more knowledge bases and aces in their arsenals.

completely, hundred percent mad today. Now go away, and do not go bothering me with your ideas of what children should be taught and what they should not! I know best, I have experience."

And she was my best friend! Ah, well.

Why haven't I spoken about brain foods, you may ask. Believe me, as normal, healthy, little children, we definitely did not eat anything special for our brains, like dry fruit, – perhaps once or twice a year in festive seasons and sweet meats, but we had healthy diets, plenty of exercise, and best of all, we did not suffer from stress and tension.

The main problem why so many people think that their brains are tired is because they are physically and mentally tired. That is why, rather than exercising their brains, they would do something which does not make them feel a tension headache.

There are so many exercises thought up by researchers and Mensa level people, who are trying to prove that there are races which are considerably intelligent than other races or people of one particular region are more developed intellectually than people of other regions. Incidentally, according to them, people of their region, including them have amazing mental powers, according to their own research.

Believe me, all that is Tommy rot, all my eye and Betty Martin. Mental development and cranial superiority definitely does not depend on caste, creed, race, religion, region, color, – however much somebody is trying to prove otherwise – but more on inherited traits, gene line, nutrition, and upbringing.

On the other hand, if you find yourself sitting ever so often, despairing because your brainpower is going down, you have only yourself to blame.

The brain is not getting anything challenging to do, except spend its time either thinking of something vague, or watching some moving pictures on a screen, or assimilating a song which you have heard hundred times before. Where does it get the initiative to do something with its natural inherited abilities and force?

So, before I sign off, here is our last brain test.

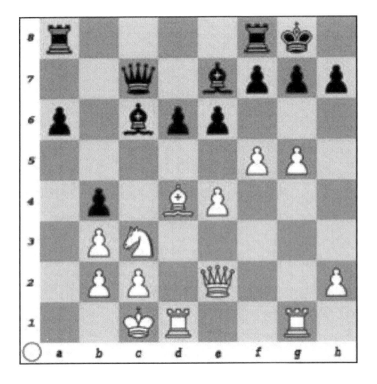

Look at this chessboard carefully for 1 minute. Look at the positions of all the chessmen.

After 1 minute, you are going to cover the chessboard and tell everybody where the white knight is. For those people who do not know about chess, it is that chessman, which looks like a horse. Which number, and which alphabet corresponds to its position?

Live Long and Prosper!

Author Bio

Dueep Jyot Singh is a Management and IT Professional who managed to gather Postgraduate qualifications in Management and English and Degrees in Science, French and Education while pursuing different enjoyable career options like being an hospital administrator, IT,SEO and HRD Database Manager/ trainer, movie , radio and TV scriptwriter, theatre artiste and public speaker, lecturer in French, Marketing and Advertising, ex-Editor of Hearts On Fire (now known as Solstice) Books Missouri USA, advice columnist and cartoonist, publisher and Aviation School trainer, ex-moderator on Medico.in, banker, student councilor ,travelogue writer … among other things!

One fine morning, she decided that she had enough of killing herself by Degrees and went back to her first love -- writing. It's more enjoyable! She already has 48 published academic and 14 fiction- in- different- genre books under her belt.

When she is not designing websites or making Graphic design illustrations for clients , she is browsing through old bookshops hunting for treasures, of which she has an enviable collection – including R.L. Stevenson, O.Henry, Dornford Yates, Maurice Walsh, De Maupassant, Victor Hugo, Sapper, C.N. Williamson, "Bartimeus" and the crown of her collection- Dickens "The Old Curiosity Shop," and "Martin Chuzzlewit" and so on… Just call her "Renaissance Woman" - collecting herbal remedies, acting like Universal Helping Hand/Agony Aunt, or escaping to her dear mountains for a bit of exploring, collecting herbs and plants, and trekking.

Check out some of the other JD-Biz Publishing books

Gardening Series on Amazon

Download Free Books!

http://MendonCottageBooks.com

Health Learning Series

Country Life Books

Health Learning Series

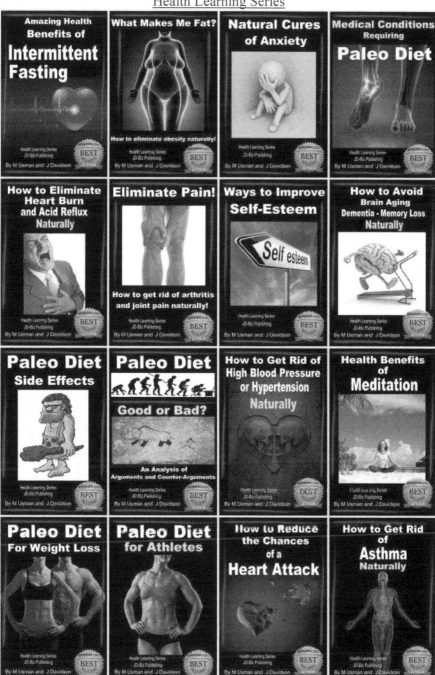

Amazing Animal Book Series

Learn To Draw Series

How to Build and Plan Books

Entrepreneur Book Series

Boost Your Memory

Our books are available at

1. Amazon.com
2. Barnes and Noble
3. Itunes
4. Kobo
5. Smashwords
6. Google Play Books

Download Free Books!

http://MendonCottageBooks.com

Publisher

JD-Biz Corp

P O Box 374

Mendon, Utah 84325

http://www.jd-biz.com/

Printed in Great Britain
by Amazon